INNOVATIVE LEADERSHIP

A Leadership Resource For Leaders of Leaders
Accompanying Bonus:
52 week Inspirational Therapy Program

by Ced Reynolds
Certified Inspirational Therapist

ISBN-13:978-1511858786
ISBN-10:1511858788

Dedication

I want to dedicate Innovative Leadership to three people who mean the world to me. My mother Essie Reed, who has always inspired me to dream big. My son Cedric James Reynolds, who always reminds me how gifted I am. My mother-in-love, Jessie Booker, who believes in me like her own son.

Table of Contents

Acknowledgements

There is no way this book even gets written without the coming together of the Single and Not Ashamed Facebook group and ministry. The initial leaders, David Burrus, Christine Gates, Erika Adams and Kara Taylor were instrumental in the development of the mission statement of SANA which includes innovative leadership as a key component. Their contribution to my life as a leader blesses me to no end.

Over the the last 21 years, ministerial leaders in the Foursquare movement such as Paul Risser, Glenn Burris, Jack Hayford and Kimberly and Jerry Dirmann have been so invaluable through their personal examples and encouragement. I appreciate everyone of them immensely.

There has been a host of friends and ministry associates who have just always had an encouraging word for me at the right time. The ones listed here are extremely special to me. Joe Valery, Regina Clay, Adolf and Rachel Pacheco, Regina Baker and Rochelle Howard.

Lastly, there are two special groups of people who give me a reason to get up everyday. CentrePoint Christian Fellowship is the congregation I have served as pastor since 1994. The other group is the Single and Not Ashamed Group which has some of the most awesome single folks in the world.

Chapter 1
Innovation

When I first started talking about innovative leadership among the people that I have connected with recently here in the business that I am engaged in, it became something that wasn't far fetched at all. The reason is because a lot of people have already heard about Innovative Leadership in reference to ministry and how we utilize it in our own personal lives.

What made Innovative Leadership become something a little bit more fascinating is the ministry component and leaders can get really innovative when it comes to leading leaders. Often we talk about creativity in the area of ministry. Creativity and innovation are totally different because one is when you create from basically nothing but innovation is already a state which already exists and you begin to make it better.

Perhaps it's a fifty year old situation or something that you see for the future. As I began to look at the different things in reference to leadership, I used to say I am a creator. In reality I am more of an innovator because I look at existing situations and try to find ways to make them better. I am one that has a heart to see that which already exists and make it better, especially when it comes to working with other leaders.

I find some people have a tendency to think like me to some degree but they are not realizing that innovation is something that they already do. They can actually participate by taking the very thing that they are already doing and finding a different way to do it, just by tweaking it a little bit.

For example we have a group that I am working that is called Single and Not Ashamed and we take some ideas such as a particular day of the week and we called it a Theme Day. Market It Monday is one of our theme days.

This theme day is regular day where we have given it a specific purpose and function to produce somewhat predictable end result. It is really nothing more than just a simple group effort that you normally see on Facebook, Google Plus or similar platforms and participants have an opportunity to promote their business and post about their books and CDs and whatever they are talking about. They do that on the page where people respond with questions and have an opportunity to get involved. We made that project innovative by taking the same exact idea that other groups use and adding a few variations to create more activity.

We decided to test the Market It Monday project on what is called an event page in our Facebook group. Initially like many new projects, there was quite an interest. It was an expected event that would show up every Monday. People loved the idea until we discovered we had one too many steps for them to participate.

There is such a thing as getting too innovative for your own good. Ask me, I know. So you are doing an event; you produce the event; you publish the event and let the people know that the event is taking place and when people show for the event, they typically are going somewhere totally different. So what we did was ask people to come for the event online through the event page. When they came to the event page, the event will primarily be a business event.

We will also offer opportunity for people to be involved and this particular event that would allow them to advertise their business and look at other businesses if they choose to and begin to participate in that particular event on the event page. So that is the innovative aspect of it.

Sometimes these things don't work the way that you want them to right? So you have to tweak a little bit and you work on both together and do things a little bit different and make certain that the people do understand because big part of it, is communication. If we are going to communicate effectively, that means we have to be willing to take the good with the bad. With this particular project, we did our research and thought we covered everything necessary to succeed.

Our discovery after launching the project let us know by the actions of the participants, they wanted and needed something different. So, what does an innovator do when there is a mishap? It's back to the drawing board like anybody else.

Change is nothing new to an innovator. Changing back to an original idea with a few tweaks is what we eventually did to get our Market It Monday back and flowing at a good pace to start an upward climb.

So we came back to where the activity is which allows people to participate in Market It Monday now with greater potential for better results. It is still the same ads; it's still the same content they have seen before but it is now all in one place. You may not understand everything I have been talking about at this very moment but one too many steps can ruin an innovative idea. Take away that step and wow, success.

One thing that happened with Market It Monday is, it only took one less step to make it happen on a regular Facebook page or group page where you just promote right there. So that is an example of an innovative leadership idea started, tweaked and restarted and retweaked.

I am an entrepreneur and a pastor and people call me the entrepreneurial pastor. It is a self proclaimed title but what I have done over the years is that I have taken simple ideas- and again I am not that creative. People say you are such a creative guy.

I have had a lot of flops and a lot of things that have gone sideways, upside down, you name it and it has been able to work out. And even back in college, when I was just a freshman, I began to monetize my innovative endeavors. It was during basketball season that my roommates and I decided it would be a good idea to get the student body some T-shirts. We said, "you know we can make this more fun, more exciting and even make some money." This was back in the days, HEAT WAVE was a popular album. The album had a wonderful cover on it that we thought would be a great design for a T-shirt. One of our roommates had access to a silk screen used by the school to print school stuff. We made the brilliant decision to use the school property to begin to produce a T-shirt that said "HEAT WAVE" on it along with our school slogan name. Needless to say, the T-shirts were a big hit until the school officials eventually found out about the product.

What was so innovative about that? Well, the innovation was we just used it for our personal benefit right? But that was not the thing we were supposed to do. So that is one of the first times I recognized innovation was a part of my life. The greater news is it became something I really enjoyed many years of my life. I was involved in selling products going directly to businesses and communicating with business owners and because I did that- of course I am always going to do things differently so I didn't want to be a regular sales guy- didn't want to be a regular person.

You and I know folks who were already selling something but they are constantly trying to make things happen differently from the way that the company said they should do it. Innovation gets in their blood and they sometimes find themselves in trouble. Now this is what I found myself doing. I found myself doing things that were just right close to the edge sometimes and that is not always good. You probably can see, you got to check yourself if you plan on being innovative.

Chapter 2
Door To Door

For me, the innovation bug continued to follow me when I became a dictionary salesman years ago, I sold Webster's dictionaries and also Funk and Wagnalls dictionaries. We actually went door to door trying to reach home owners during the day to no avail. One day my partner and I saw an industrial park and decided there were mothers and fathers there too. So we headed off to see them. We noticed other business to business sales people were out doing the same thing. But their angle was to talk with the business owner. Ours would be to speak with the person who was trying to keep us away from the business owner.

Now again, a lot of guys would go directly to the ones owning the businesses right? Some would even go only with the intention of speaking with the business owner. We figured the folks at the front desks, the mechanics and anybody who would greet us at the business was a candidate for a dictionary. Makes lot of sense right? So that is what we did. My partner and I went to the businesses in the community recognizing they were working and were concerned about their children. We would walk in and talk to them about dictionaries. We had what we thought was a great presentation that was extremely professional. We had people crowding around us just to watch our presentation because we were just that professional and entertaining. What we did was unheard of. People thought we had this wonderful thing going on and we just talked about our particular product in an innovative way. We got them to begin to participate with us as well.

We understood what crowd participation was. We knew special crowd participation would be getting people involved in the show from an emotional perspective as well as a benefits perspective. We also got them committed to make a purchase and receive delivery.

My partner and I were ready to make some money for ourselves so that was really a powerful time for our business. We didn't even have a full idea of what we were doing but as we did so, we found ourselves putting on a show that went on for a while and people were buying dictionaries all over the place and we were delivering dictionaries all over the place, which was fantastic. That innovative aspect of our business has kept us in a position where we were comfortable. Now when we began to hire employees, people that we wanted to begin to do things like us.

We found sometimes that innovation didn't work as effectively as we initially thought it would. That was a tough thing to really swallow because when we presented our product in the marketplace, it worked fine. As innovative as I thought I was, I realized that my partner was innovative in a different way than I was. We had a lot to learn from each other.

The innovation that we often headed individually was so much different because of our own personal styles. My style was somewhat conservative but because I was concerned with even our dress code, people were looking at me like just a dry guy that was just part of the duo.

But when the show was on, we both would be making things happen. I began to come alive and our innovative presentation was good to go. As much as we would like to believe everybody appreciates innovation, not everybody is moved by innovation or doing innovative things.

We came to realize that not everybody goes with the flow. We all need times in our lives where we discover some of the things we do effectively and find the ones that do work and work for our audience as well. That's when what we're doing at that instance is innovation.

Chapter 3
Leverage

I will talk a little bit about innovation here more maturely because this is something that has really strengthened me a lot because it's caused me to watch people now even in the ministry getting more innovative.

People have begun to identify a little more with me because they are not looking for the same old, same old. People who have been involved in church life for a long time have become stuck doing the same things year after year. Church is the same. Bible Studies are the same. Annual activities are the same. There's just limited change with the same old limited results.

Take prayer meetings for instance. A church or ministry can call prayer for a specific time and very few people show up. I would say the the reason they don't show up is because of the commute and the overall time commitment. Done in a more innovative way a church or ministry can effectively have prayer via the phone or using online platforms such as FreeConferenceCall.com, Skype or Talkshoe.com.

It's a simple thing using a telephone to have prayer. It's as simple as repurposing the use of the platforms for prayer rather than business phone calls. To have group prayer with people early in the morning and when they are up and about getting ready for their day and getting ready to move out to their work place; having a specific time of prayer is an innovative way to use a phone.

You might not think that may be a really big deal but that is something that we do right now. We actually pray with groups of people on the phone. Now please understand this, we don't pray innovatively. We pray according to the Bible. What is innovative is our use of the phone to accomplish something that it wasn't actually designed for specifically. It's innovative also because people participate without having to meet at a location other than be on their own telephone.

Now the main thing about it is that we have people all over the country who are joining us because they are now able to get on the phone 24/7, same time different time zone but they are able to get on the phone and pray with us as well so you can see where innovation becomes very useful. Now you are not just involved with people who are local but you are involved with people around the country who are able to get on the phone and pray the same time; so that is just a simple innovative idea that came up in something we have been doing for many years now. On top of all of this, recordings of the calls can be made for those who miss the prayer calls can listen to at their convenience.

Innovation is very important when it comes to leverage. We leveraged what we were already doing. It was more than just me praying with a few people by myself at my church. In my mind I would think it would be a whole lot more sensible to actually pray on the phone for an hour than to go to church pray with the people of the church and drive back home. During this season, I figured it out that it is okay that I can go to church be on the phone and pray with the same people after church and I can pray with people there at the church as well as pray with people on the phone. That was great too, but then my commute from home increased in distance, and I began to think of a better way to serve the people who wanted to pray.

So what happened was that I began to pray at home with the same people that wanted to pray with me no matter if they were at home or not. I would pray with them as well, on the phone and all around the country at the same time. That innovative idea saved time and saved me a lot of energy. Certainly it did and because of that I was able to find myself doing a much better prayer and it made things so much more simple.

Chapter 4
Implementation

I am telling you today that innovation is one wonderful thing if you are able to take advantage of it by doing it yourself. I will encourage you to be involved as the person that is innovative not just spending time doing what you feel like doing on your own but doing it in an innovative manner that will get you moving in a good direction.

Some of the ideas that I will share with you today are really pretty simple. They are not complicated at all. All I will do is take a simple idea that already exists and add another idea to it or take an idea from it and do it in a different way. Hopefully you'll see the benefits involved at the end of the day. These will be some of the things that I have been doing online recently.

I am going to be talking to you about innovation in various capacities. More than just business and ministry but also your personal life as well. I will give you some idea about what you can do to take your life to another level. Some of you happen to be in business for yourself, some are in ministry and some are just exploring some options that you want to have in your life that - you have some ideas but you are not sure how to begin to implement them. Implementation is a big part of anything. If I would get into anything right now, it would be about implementation because a few minutes ago we talked about implementation and that really means that I am going to take the time to find out how to do something right now.

What stops you from implementing anything effectively? The first word you might think about is fear. Fear of the unknown. Not knowing exactly what is going to happen; not knowing how it was going to happen; not knowing if it was going to work out right at all. Here is a reality for you. We are not always sure things are going to work out all the time but we do give it a try anyway. We do as much as we can as far as research is concerned. We do as much as we can, as far as getting an understanding about our innovative idea is concern and a little understanding of what is already working.

Sometimes it may not be necessary to innovate. It may not be as necessary to because there are things that are actually working already. We don't just innovate just to be innovative. I want you to understand that too. I just don't innovate because I want to be innovative. The reason I innovate is because I see a better way to do it.

I see the way that it is currently being done as good but I see that there has to be a better way. If you are not sold on the idea of it being necessary to innovate; you will not implement effectively. But when you are sold on the idea you will find a way to implement it. You really will, even if that means you will fail a lot of time to achieve.

I have been in a situation where I tried several times just to get to the point where I can get the thing done correctly. It didn't mean that I did bad research. I just had to go through a few processes so that I could get a better understanding so when I finally got to the place where I begin to implement I would see things more effectively. I saw the outcome that I wanted to see as well. And when you get this outcome you want to see, you say my goodness, "it finally did work effectively that way."

One of the newest projects we have going right now is what we are doing with relationships. So we have relationships that we talk about on our Facebook group sponsored radio program. We also have a private Facebook group where we talk are relationship topics. Although both projects talk about relationships, they are supportive of one another. While the radio show is live, the Relationship Group posts comments and makes responses. The innovation here is the way they go about interacting with each other being on separate platforms. In fact, they are on multiple platforms at once. The internet, the phone and a mobile app, coinciding with each other at the same time. So, while the radio show is going on live around the world, the Facebook group is a private group that people connect with and listen to the radio program and they dialogue about what is happening on the radio-program.

This is not something that happens all the time. So they are now together connected with their project and it makes it work in a very effective way. So those are just some of the things we have implemented. It was just something that I said: okay now, can these platforms work together? I said yes and then I began to implement it and gave instruction along the way and that people would be able to identify this is going to be coming. The community would see a note like this, by the way guys, we are going to have a radio program- we have this wonderful thing happening- am talking about this from the radio perspective; then I go over to the Facebook Relationship group and talk about it in the Facebook group: we are going to have a live radio program posted with a hot topic on relationships in our Facebook page tonight.

Implementation makes a major difference and that is what we begin to do. We start implementing ideas we believe are going to work effectively.

Chapter 5
Strategy

Now, as we moved beyond just the area of innovative leadership and just having these wild crazy ideas, we began to think about strategy. This is when we really started putting together something on purpose. We went the extra mile of not just doing it well in our own sight but in the sight of others. The strategic ideas now are more than throwing something against the wall and see what sticks.

When any of us choose to succeed, we give up on the idea of failure being an option. We choose to hone our skills and develop a method of operation that works with a degree of certainty (at least for a while). We call it a formula. If you will have formula on how to implement certain things, you are able to position yourself on purpose and work strategically on a daily basis. Writing this book is all about doing things in a systematic manner, working on a daily basis and measuring my activity. I have a strategy on how I am doing the book; it's not just a matter of me just throwing some words together; some numbers together or writing some things out.

I have given some illustrations that show actual innovative ideas that have been successfully implemented so you have an understanding about how I got to this point- how I moved from point to point. You get chance to see innovative ideas. You get a chance to see how the ideas were implemented. You get a chance to get a glimpse of the strategies used in implementation. All in all, you were able to experience how I took projects that are working okay already and what I did to bring a little improvement to them for a result I desired.

So here is what we do-strategy wise: we talk about how we are going to now make a mark that is going to be so much different that other people will begin to take notice. Part of this strategy is getting other people to take notice so they would begin to approach you. You are looking; and always trying to be the best sales person, the person that people are always going to; the person that always stands out- the guy who is always running out to people, looking to meet their needs. You would be the person who caused people to worry less because they counted on you because of your innovative leadership.

I would post something on Facebook that I know would engage people who are already leaders and because I am able to do that I will get their responses right back. By the way that is a strategic post that would get them to respond and because I know their responses are going to be in a specific area, that also gives me insight at this point, to communicate with them a second time. So the second time I am taking them on a journey with me and because I am taking folks on a journey with me, they have a chance to be a participant in my strategic leadership.

Now, that is innovative because I am working with folks who I know are already out there watching, following me already and so when I put out information- put it out on purpose- it's not just because I felt like putting something out for a while. It was definitely on purpose.

Often I deal with people who don't understand when I sometimes talk about SANA clues (Single And Not Ashamed Clues). They are simply clues that happen to relate to people from a perspective of identifying- let's say clues in life. You know we have some clues that are really going to help people do better in life and we don't give them answers to life- but we give them clues to life.

Now every person would have a different understanding of those clues based on where they happen to be in life and no wrong answers if you will. So when I put those SANA clues out, you would be surprised by the number of people who respond to them. When they do respond I am able to identify the ones that I want to communicate with- can you see that? So that is part of the strategy in picking out people. I am actually picking people out to communicate with; picking people out that I would help to lead in their life at some point; picking people out that I would want to be on my team; to be a part of what I do.

Building a team of people when it comes to innovative leadership is extremely vital and I want to address that in the next chapter.

Chapter 6
Team Building

I told you last time that I was going to talk to you about building a team because one of the things about leverage is doing more than what you can do by yourself. Even innovative leaders need teams. It's part of thinking about how we could take something and make it better than what we can do by ourselves and I am always thinking that way all the time. I wanted to find ways to build a team and that is one of the things I do in the beginning stages.

My initial goal when I begin a new project is to have 12 people who I can connect with. My reason for that is because that is what Jesus did. He had a team of 12 guys and I look at what Jesus did as being a clue. My aim is to look for 12 people that I can connect with and then help them to build their own teams as well because everyone of them would have a unique situation when they are involved with me. They have their own calling, they have their own ability to do things and I want to help them become the best they can be.

The innovative component there is that I am not just taking 2 or 3 people to work with; I am taking 12. So everyone would be receiving from me, individual instruction, individual communication and individual attention. That is not really an easy thing to do but I believe that it is really worth while because again everyone of them have their own personality; their own styles and their own ways of doing what they do. The one thing that most of them would have, is some sort of innovative capacity about them. That is why they connect with me in the first place.

So I work with 12 people and train them to get their innovative skills really ramped up in big way. The aim is to have them do the same thing that I do in reference to building a team, being able to implement innovative ideas and to identify ways to be innovative because they believe innovation offers better solutions.

Another way we go about building teams is through the blog of our SANA community. The blog is a fascinating way to communicate because what happens here is that we give folks this wonderful opportunity to write and they get excited about it because they are writing among their peers. When they write among their peers and they have the chance to read it, their authorship begins to get noticed by people that like to read as well. That is a fun thing.

What that does to the leader of that group is that it gives her the chance to manage the people that want to write and learn more. We leverage the idea of having a blog that has more than just one person writing on the blog. Multiple people write on the blog. Multiple people promote the blog. Now it's seen on various platforms by other Singles who might want to write as well.

That is how we begin to increase the leverage there. That is how we begin to get innovative in reference to the way we are doing blogging. So it is not just one person trying to blog or people starting different blogs elsewhere. We are bringing them all together in one group and having a blog that talks about various topics in reference to the single life. So the people who happen to be single now have a chance to be in one place among people of like faith, interest, situations and circumstances and able to gather information that is going to be beneficial for their lives.

So it not just saying: come check out the blog I have some information I want to share with you but come check out the blog we have a lot of information to share with you because it is not just about me anymore. Now people are more open to share other people's content- other writers content. That makes it exciting. One of the unique things that will be occurring on that blog is you will find people that would begin to monetize the blog because now they are writing information that is viable for people but also to be able to communicate to them about how they can assist them better. They may have products that they have created such as a book, an audio series or a coaching program.

They have been able to get that information out to people and when they do that people are able to gather information; purchase their book or audio series or whatever other resources that they might have and because of that they are able to earn an income at the same time. So you can see with innovation, we created the platform where we are giving some a chance to move beyond being there by themselves or going to do their own blog all by themselves. We have become innovative about it and put all these people together at the same place. They now have a greater degree of confidence; they have a commonality of interest and reference to them being single and they are writing about different subject matters but even more because more people are coming as a result of being in a singles world. That is one of the ways we talk about innovative leadership in reference to team building.

Team building is extremely valuable for every group and often we don't talk about team building when it comes to innovative leadership because we think the idea of innovative leadership requires one person to lead. I think we should always be on the lookout for leaders to lead because- listen, I lead leaders. I find leaders who are leading already and then help them to lead more effectively. If I can do that over and over and over again we will see multitude of leaders leading leaders and that is going to be a more dynamic situation that would occur more-so, than me trying to lead all the people myself and that's definitely not the thing for me.

Jesus worked with guys and He told them He was going to make them fishers of men. He said: follow Me and I am going to make you fishers of men. He wasn't just talking to some guys that were broke; he is talking to some guys that were fishermen already. They were already doing well and so he helped them become leaders in a better capacity. That is the same thing that I am looking to do. I want to model Jesus and take my innovative leadership skills to another level.

We talked about the leveraging component in chapter 3. Can you see now through the example of Jesus, how this is such a powerful component in the area of innovative leadership? So many people are looking to do better in life so what do they do about it? They find people that can help. What do I do as a leader? I identify those people looking for leadership. There are many people in the world that say they are looking for leadership but are not really ready because it does require commitment on the person's part to be led. So my job now is that I identify those people who are looking to be led. These are the ones I have identified already are looking to be led. People know within themselves that they really want to be led. They want to be led by somebody who is innovative and making things happen.

So those are just some of the team building ideas that we have actually begun to implement as far as innovative leadership is concerned. So people can begin to see things that are actually working because you can see the innovation without having to look really hard. I can see exactly what they have done here. The innovation is so much different. Now you have to keep this next real time innovative idea in mind. We have a group of singles that happen to be younger adults between 18 – early 30ish. The younger adults are part of our primary SANA group which the age ranges are around 35 – 45. We even have a few folks my age (55).

I get this inbox message from one of our young adults about an idea. You know, I love fresh new ideas. His idea was to form a new online group specifically for young adults. Now he could have just done this on his own but he wanted to remain as a member of SANA because of the positive nature of the group.

So, I ask him to put together a proposal and he does. Wow, what an amazing idea to connect with fellow single young adults who are looking to live out their singleness in a godly manner. Once in a while one of our SANA leaders pops in to give a word of encouragement to the group just to stay connected. Here's the joy. The group was started by young adults for young adults and it's still part of the primary group. What often happens is a group gets formed in secret and the leader is the last to know part of the team has defected. In this case, the young adult leader felt comfortable enough to contact me and voice his thoughts and we got the ball rolling. It's cool to relate well enough to others and they realize that I have this innovative way of thinking that they are willing to approach me with innovative ideas about how to implement.

Can you see the kind of people I'm looking for? Could you do me a favor? Could you help me find more ways to find more people to help me help them implement innovative ideas? That's right, I am looking for people who have ideas that are innovative. When people approach me with innovative ideas, I want them it to sell me; I want them to really explain to me that they have something that's different and tell me why and if they can tell me why their idea is innovative and are not afraid, we will really have a great conversation. Often people approach a leader with a bit of inner fear because they are not sure if the leader is going to really receive it or not.

I like the 27 year old who approached me and said, "I have got this idea about our group- I love the group, it is so fantastic but the reality is that we've got some young people here that may not be as close to understanding what's really going on here as I am and I really want to help them because I can see them being able to be helped effectively." Today that team exists because of the innovative leadership of one man. Isn't that great?

Of course he began to write his ideas down and of course we talked about it a little bit more and identified that it's a definite need. We took an idea that already existed and twisted it a little bit and found out a way to get it to the people that were really going to receive it and give them the information that they need to have in a way they can receive it-that's innovation. So that one idea right there by one young person has been able to open-up a door where other young people would be able to be blessed by God because they are desiring something that they didn't know they even needed. Now they were able to share with others in an innovative way and that's where I look at it and go wow! It's worth it because it's not just me coming up with innovative ideas anymore, it's other people. That is when you get really excited.

Now some of these are people I haven't even chosen as leaders. This guy just saw there is opportunity here and so I have to keep my eyes and ears open for people who are already thinking like I am thinking but I don't even know it. So not knowing everybody is okay but at some point you have to open-up your ears and your eyes and hear this by the way. Sometimes you have to let them know that it's not for you. I appreciate what you have offered but it's not good yet. Another way we look at things as well is how the innovator/innovators team-up with other people that are innovative but are really what I call a support people and support people really help the innovators because they come alongside to bring a little bit of a sticky component towards that innovative leader.

Now this is how that works- one of the teams we have, happens to support women. It is a women's ministry that does it by phone and again using the phone is vital and they do it by phoning and ministering to these ladies by phone and one of the ideas was simply this: why don't we have a Facebook group that works with the women after they have been ministered to and care for them in the Facebook group or private group that cares for these ladies by answering questions, nurturing them and even getting on the phone further if we have to. That's another innovative idea.

Heartfelt ideas is where innovation begins to work. The love that people have for other people is what causes an innovator to come up with viable solutions to the issues of certain people. We kind of give them that internal vision and that internal vision makes us think that we have the whole idea- often we don't have the whole idea; that's why innovation will always be necessary. That's why one idea that somebody had about doing something in this particular way has been done in an entirely different way. It's been repurposed and we are just demonstrating ways of doing what we do. Repurposing them so that it can be done effectively to help other people and at the end of the day what we are looking for is helping people's lives change because we want to see other people's lives affected in a way that they have not been affected before.

Okay, I hope you're saying by now, "well if they can do this, I can do this and so can anybody else who wants to." Well, the ideas I am talking about are simply thoughts of people who have had the heart to really step-up to the plate and do something different because they know that the ways that things have then been done is not working. When things are not working effectively, somebody has to make a difference by making a change. If you feel compelled to make that kind of change, perhaps you are an innovative leader..

Chapter 7
Innovation and You

Let me talk to you about you for a moment.

I'm not sure why you purchased this book. I'm not sure if you would even consider yourself innovative. I do have a strong suspicion that you are a leader though.

I do want to challenge you to look back over your life first of all and identify where you have been, who you have been with and the type of things you have done- because if you have been involved in innovation to any degree you would know it.

Perhaps as a small child you probably saw your friends or even participated in skateboarding yourself. Many of my friends, including girls had skateboards when I was a kid. One thing that was fairly common among all of us was most of us broke our skateboards. Of course our parents weren't made of money so there weren't many of us who got replacement skateboards. So what did we do? We got innovative.

Remember the shopping carts at the grocery stores? Those wheels were a perfect fit to make skateboards. They were just really tricky to control. Here's what we did. We took the wheels from the shopping carts, found flat wood surface to use as a board and as an added bonus, we added a wooden handle to help us steer better. So in essence we upgraded to a scooter. Now, that's innovation. Albeit, a little dicey (forgive me) but innovation nonetheless. If you did that kind of thing as a child maybe you have a little innovation in you as well.

Now, we weren't even thinking innovation back in those days. We were just thinking about how we would get around. The innovation and the boldness just came based on our perceived need and believing we had no other options.

Think about what you did with your dolls ladies. Perhaps you decided instead of having just a plain old doll, you would put on different kind of clothes on your doll. Put the doll in a bear suit or whatever you had. All you were looking for was something different, fun and exciting. Something that really got you motivated.

Maybe it was reading that you really enjoyed so much you decided to do something different to make yourself be a little more innovative when it came to reading. Then doing your history assignment became one of the things that happen to be in school and you made it fun for yourself. You see, you were the person who really functioned innovatively and didn't even know it during the time because the personal benefit that came was a result of doing something different that you had never done before and other people had the chance to watch you.

Now, watch this part; now other people having the chance to watch you, gave you the insight that: hmm! Maybe I am doing something pretty smart here and then you are able to start monetizing that very same thing of innovative leadership. We find ways to earn an income from it, you start selling newspapers and instead of selling newspapers to people door to door you begin to call them on the phone and say: hey listen I have got some newspapers for sale that I will be dropping by in the morning, my mom and dad will be helping me get the papers out, I would like to drop one by for you guys as well. Would you like to have one for your home or one for work? I will be happy to bring you two. You see, that's innovative because you are thinking a little bit different; you thinking outside the box rather than again just talking to people about one thing, you're talking to them about two different things at the same time.

You can be the popular teacher on campus by taking a newspaper to your classroom and keeping one for home as well. Be the one that's going take a newspaper to the donut shop when you stop at the donut shop and be the one that's going to bring you goodwill when you go to work. You see that's innovative- that's just being different. It just takes a little bit of thought to be innovative. So if you are thinking in terms like that, you are an innovative person. I hope that would encourage you to reread this book and to identify where you happen to be in your life, what you have done in the past, what you are doing now and how your future could be if you begin to implement innovative leadership. If you're a leader of leaders, consider building a team of people that implement innovative leadership principles.

This is what I have done by writing this book. By writing this book, I have been able to provide information to people and give them the chance to be able to identify that they can be an innovative leader also. It's not by being so super smart but just by identifying where they happen to be in life and what they want to accomplish.

I have been innovative all my life and I didn't even know it until people started asking me to do things that I have never done before. I have been able to do stuff that I have never thought about doing before just because I think a little bit differently and I found out that my thinking is okay. You are a fantastic individual that has some ideas that are a little bit different than most people think about because you have those thoughts and ideas.

Don't you think that God gave you those ideas for his purposes? Don't you think that God placed you in this world for his purposes? Don't you think that God gave you some insight on something so you can get things accomplished for his kingdom? So here's what I am going tell you right now. My innovative leadership is designed to help you as a person. So I have helped you identify that things can be done on a secular scale and in the ministry if you chose to. It could be done in various kinds of ways but I am also encouraging you that in your own personal purpose in life, right now that God wants to use you to be able to bring glory to his kingdom by being innovative. Imagine the things that would happen in the kingdom of God as a result of us desiring to be innovative in our leadership.

The world is looking for leaders right now; the world is starving for good genuine people who want to lead effectively. The world is starving for people who are doing a work for the kingdom's sake. The world is starving for people like you and I all day long every day, so I have chosen to wake up. I have chosen to be one that's going to be upfront. I have chosen to be one that's going to say: okay team let's go build a team of folks here. I have chosen to be one that says, okay, I'll write the book. Okay, I'll put the book out. I'll do that. Okay, I have chosen to challenge you to help me leverage the message of spreading the gospel of Jesus Christ via your own personal innovative project. That's simply to get the word of God out in the unique way that you do it. That's to get the people of the world to recognize that you are a Christian.

Perhaps you are not a Christian. Perhaps you are just reading this book today and you are seeing yourself as a person who is just in need of this type of innovation in your life and you are not sure how to get it.

Listen, I don't want to take a lot of your time but I would like to help you become a better innovator by introducing you to the innovator of innovators. The same man I spoke of earlier in the book who helped a few fishermen and business leaders become fishers of men can help you.

Like every man, He has a story. His is quite unique. Unlike most men, He lived a life without ever cursing His neighbor, He never crossed a friend, He never fornicated...

He was the kind of Man every Father would love to have. He obeyed His Father all 33 years of His life. The ironic thing about His life is He was able to help so many people with His innovative ways of doing things. The way He functioned was so much different than people of His generation and the generations behind and yet to come.

All in all, the story of this Man goes really deep. To make it short and to the point, this Man was born in an innovative manner, He lived in an innovative manner and He died in an innovative manner.

Everything that Jesus Christ did, He did for you and me so that we could live a life full of purpose. If today, you see your life empty of purpose and void of life worth telling people about, let me introduce you to Jesus Christ. He will literally save your life.

> The word that saves is right here,
> as near as the tongue in your mouth,
> as close as the heart in your chest.

It's the word of faith that welcomes God to go to work and set things right for us. This is the core of our preaching. Say the welcoming word to God—"Jesus is my Master"—embracing, body and soul, God's work of doing in us what he did in raising Jesus from the dead. That's it. You're not "doing" anything; you're simply calling out to God, trusting him to do it for you. That's salvation. With your whole being you embrace God setting things right, and then you say it, right out loud: "God has set everything right between him and me! Romans 10:9-10 The Message Bible

_____

Sign above if everything is okay between you and God

_____

Date

Welcome To the Family of God

52 Week Inspirational Therapy Guide

First of all, let me answer the question, why 52 weeks? The reality is doing devotionals everyday, people have a tendency to miss a day or two every now and then. So I decided to put together something a person could concentrate on for the entire week. It's just that simple.

The reason we call this an inspirational therapy guide is because the content you will see comes directly from a leadership campaign called Single And Not Ashamed. It's simply a project for single men and women who are not ashamed of the gospel of Christ and have a strong interest in being used by God now in their singleness. No worries, if you're married, the inspirational therapy guide can still be used by you.

Over the years I've always shared my thoughts on my social media pages. Most of the time it's been Quotes From My Heart which is an e-book I've written. Ever since I founded the Single And Not Ashamed Facebook Group, I've continued to share what I believe are biblical truths in the form of a quote with or without scripture.

The instructions are pretty brief. Every week, you will ponder the weekly quote. Upon pondering the quote, you will write out your initial observation about the quote. Secondly, you will write out how you will apply what you've observed about the quote in your life.

The aim is to give you the opportunity to practice gaining inspiration from what you eventually read on a daily basis. You can take the full 52 weeks or read, write an observation and write an application in as short a time as you wish.

I do hope you enjoy your discovery using this Inspirational Therapy Guide.

Inspirational Therapy Week One

Jesus didn't force anybody to follow Him. His commanding presence compelled men to follow Him.

Personal Observation:

Personal Application:

Inspirational Therapy Week Two

Believing God can, even when we can't see how it's possible, is better than believing He might, when we've seen Him do it before.

Personal Observation:

Personal Application:

Inspirational Therapy Week Three

God didn't make us to eat from the crumbs off of His table. He organized the banquet just for us.

Personal Observation:

Personal Application:

Inspirational Therapy Week Four

Normal leadership is the ability to influence followers to follow. Innovative leadership is the ability to influence leaders to lead.

Personal Observation:

Personal Application:

Inspirational Therapy Week Five
After a man submits to God, he must then learn to submit to the man of God who watches over his soul.

Personal Observation:

Personal Application:

Inspirational Therapy Week Six

Secure men willingly submit to men of like faith because they realize the benefit of mutual submission.

Personal Observation:

Personal Application:

Inspirational Therapy Week Seven

Leaders who love God and love themselves, find it easier to love those they lead.

Personal Observation:

Personal Application:

Inspirational Therapy Week Eight

The greater joy of a leader, is watching the leaders they influence, influence other leaders, influencing other leaders.

Personal Observation:

Personal Application:

Inspirational Therapy Week Nine
Leaders set you up to win when they see you're running in the right direction.

Personal Observation:

Personal Application:

Inspirational Therapy Week Ten

Although leaders lead with intention and conviction, they realize God's grace is sufficient.

Personal Observation:

Personal Application:

Inspirational Therapy Week Eleven
Leaders who lead well will eventually help you look better than them.

Personal Observation:

Personal Application:

Inspirational Therapy Week Twelve
Leaders led by the Spirit with the same message is a God thing. Catch the meaning.

Personal Observation:

Personal Application:

Inspirational Therapy Week Thirteen
When leaders show up in one accord, the Lord is demonstrating His purpose for those who will take heed

Personal Observation

Personal Application:

Inspirational Therapy Week Fourteen
Contagious leadership will transform your
communities. Just let it flow.

Personal Observation:

Personal Application:

Inspirational Therapy Week Fifteen
Leaders recognize God's grace makes them look better than they really are.

Personal Observation:

Personal Application:

Inspirational Therapy Week Sixteen
Leaders lead by faith because they know it pleases God.

Personal Observation:

Personal Application:

Inspirational Therapy Week Seventeen
All leaders fail. It's the ones who pick themselves up and lead again who succeed.

Personal Observation:

Personal Application:

Inspirational Therapy Week Eighteen
A woman who truly seeks God will only follow a man who is led by God, leads himself and others well.

Personal Observation:

Personal Application:

Inspirational Therapy Week Nineteen
Men who refuse to be led will have few followers.
Leaders are led too.

Personal Observation:

Personal Application:

Inspirational Therapy Week Twenty
Leaders lead in crisis just like they lead in good times.

Personal Observation:

Personal Application:

Inspirational Therapy Week Twenty One
Leaders have an uncanny ability to lead even when they are not in charge.

Personal Observation:

Personal Application:

Inspirational Therapy Week Twenty Two

BTW, there is nothing wrong with you. You just happen to be part of a Royal Family where you are an heir of God and a joint heir with Jesus Christ.

Personal Observation:

Personal Application:

Inspirational Therapy Week Twenty Three
When you break away from the pack, don't expect everybody to embrace you. You've just stepped away from the norm.

Personal Observation:

Personal Application:

Inspirational Therapy Week Twenty Four

The mature believer didn't wake up mature. They just stayed the course of discipline long enough and realized how smart it was to continue on a disciplined road.

Personal Observation:

Personal Application:

Inspirational Therapy Week Twenty Five

Give a child what they want, when they want it, every time they want it, and you'll end up with a spoiled child. Do the same for an adult and they will end up spiritually anemic.

Personal Observation:

Personal Application:

Inspirational Therapy Week Twenty Six

A conflicted soul seeks to obey the truth and please the flesh at the same time. Deliverance is crucial.

Personal Observation:

Personal Application:

Inspirational Therapy Twenty Seven

Unchallenged faith is useless. It's faith that is active that pleases God.

Personal Observation:

Personal Application:

Inspirational Therapy Week Twenty Eight
The fervent red hot word of the Lord is what starts a fire in your soul that is never quenched. Keep the fire burning.

Personal Observation:

Personal Application:

Inspirational Therapy Week Twenty Nine
The truth endures through all generations but it only sets those free who know it.

Personal Observation:

Personal Application:

Inspirational Therapy Week Thirty

When the TRUTH resonates with your spirit, know that God has given it to you for His purpose.

Personal Observation:

Personal Application:

Inspirational Therapy Week Thirty One
Leaders who lead like Jesus, rely on the life changing word of God for EVERYTHING

Personal Observation:

Personal Application:

Inspirational Therapy Thirty Two
The word of an anointed leader spoken in season will compel you to move on a word confirmed in your spirit

Personal Observation:

Personal Application:

Inspirational Therapy Thirty Three

Kingdom leaders help you see yourself the way God sees you. Then they help you to be the way God wants you to be.

Personal Observation:

Personal Application:

Inspirational Therapy Week Thirty Four
One reason leaders emerge to the top, is because they have been at the bottom long enough to understand the true needs of the people they will eventually lead

Personal Observation:

Personal Application:

Inspirational Therapy Week Thirty Five
Jesus didn't approach beggars to follow Him. He approached leaders.

Personal Observation:

Personal Application:

Inspirational Therapy Week Thirty Six
Sometimes leaders don't say PLEASE. They just say
follow Me and I will make you fishers of men.

Personal Observation:

Personal Application:

Inspirational Therapy Week Thirty Seven
Leaders with a demanding presence get things done by requiring service on demand. Leaders with a commanding presence get things because of who they are commands respect.

Personal Observation:

Personal Application:

Inspirational Therapy Week Thirty Eight
Jesus found men who were about their own businesses and discipled them to be about His Father's business.

Personal Observation:

Personal Application:

Inspirational Therapy Week Thirty Nine
If Jesus led people in the direction they wanted to go, their eternal outcome would be so much different.

Personal Observation:

Personal Application:

Inspirational Therapy Week Forty
If hard work was enough to succeed, the sufficiency of God's grace would be irrelevant.

Personal Observation:

Personal Application:

Inspirational Therapy Week Forty One

If you only knew what God has been preparing you for, you wouldn't settle for anything less than His best.

Personal Observation:

Personal Application:

Inspirational Therapy Week Forty Two

Second chances have lots of relatives. Thank God for third, fourth, fifth, sixth, seventh and more chances.

Personal Observation:

Personal Application:

Inspirational Therapy Week Forty Three

Being in love with the idea of being in love is just another form of lust disguised. Love the idea of being in love or love God and love yourself.

Personal Observation:

Personal Application:

Inspirational Therapy Week Forty Four
Sometimes fear appears like faith because of its
sense of urgency. The difference is, faith works by
love and fear works by a misinterpretation of the love.

Personal Observation:

Personal Application:

Inspirational Therapy Forty Five

Fear of loss will have you going in every direction to lead you away from loving God and loving yourself.

Personal Observation:

Personal Application:

Inspirational Therapy Week Forty Six

Once you've said I DO, you've just said I DO to everything known and unknown.

Personal Observation:

Personal Application:

Inspirational Therapy Week Forty Seven

So you just received a word of the Lord that will change your life. Now, your job is to get to know that word and love it into manifestation.

Personal Observation:

Personal Application:

Inspirational Therapy Week Forty Eight

Perhaps you've been doing all the right stuff and life still seems to be missing something. You're walking by faith and not by sight. We don't look for the things that are seen but the things that are not seen. The things we're looking for are eternal things not temporal things.

Personal Observation:

Personal Application:

Inspirational Therapy Week Forty Nine
Your public character vs. Your private character.
Which one is the real you? Time will tell.

Personal Observation:

Personal Application:

Inspirational Therapy Week Fifty
Leaving 'poorer and sickness' out of your wedding vows doesn't exempt you from keeping the covenant should sickness or poverty strike your marriage.

Personal Observation:

Personal Application:

Inspirational Therapy Week Fifty One

Conversations and testimonies of other covenant keepers are good. They pale in comparison to living with and keeping your own covenant.

Personal Observation:

Personal Application:

Inspirational Therapy Week Fifty Two

You don't have to be perfect to keep covenant. You just have to keep it.

Personal Observation:

Personal Application:

www.ingramcontent.com/pod-product-compliance
Lightning Source LLC
Chambersburg PA
CBHW070841180526
45168CB00002B/907